UNGAINLY
THINGS

also by Robert Wallace:

VIEWS FROM A FERRIS WHEEL

POEMS ON POETRY (co-editor)

UNGAINLY THINGS

poems

by Robert Wallace

E. P. Dutton & Co., Inc. ■ *New York* ■ *1968*

Some of these poems have appeared in periodicals, to whose
editors I make grateful acknowledgment, as follows:

AMERICAN WEAVE: "The Poets"; "*Aubade*: N.Y.C."
ANTIOCH REVIEW: "Seal on an Island-Rock"; "Post-Watching:
    Little Night Heron"; "Mammoth's Journey"; "Fable";
    "Out for Stars"; "Climbing at Gay Head"; "Passage"
APPROACH: "Lines for a Discouraged Friend Digging in His Garden";
    "Susan"
CAPE ROCK QUARTERLY: "After Parting"
COMMONWEAL: "From Across the Bay"; "After the Swimmer"
EPOCH: "Birds and the Moonlight"; "Cape Cod in March"
HARPER'S MAGAZINE: "It"; "The Armadillo" (as "The Dictionary
    Armadillo")
THE NEW YORKER: "Ballad of the Mouse"; "Fly in December";
    "In the Field Forever"; © 1965, 1967, by The New Yorker
    Magazine, Inc.
THE NEW YORK TIMES: "Between Equals"; "The Saturday Morning
    of Lemuel Hill"
POETRY: "An Epitaph" (as "A Poet's Epitaph"); "For Lawson and
    Ann"; © 1967 by The Modern Poetry Association
POETRY NORTHWEST: "By the Salt Inlet"
POLEMIC: "The Body Waking"
THE REPORTER: "Ungainly Things"; "The Turtle"; "Moving";
    "Love Poem"

SATURDAY REVIEW: "Giacometti's Dog"; "For the Season";
    "Little by Little"; "Taking Back"
THE SOUTHERN REVIEW: "What Music Says"; "First Snow"; "On the
    College Archery Range"
THE VIRGINIA QUARTERLY REVIEW: "Parable for Governors";
    "The Jaguar" (as "The Dictionary Jaguar"); "Among the
    Piles of Street-Light"; "In Winter"

"Susan" was awarded a Katherine and Elizabeth Bragdon
Poetry Award in 1965.

The creatures of "The Dictionary Zoo" may be found in the
pages of *The American College Dictionary*.

for Jan,
for Mom,
who bound my world

Contents

1

Giacometti's Dog

lopes in bronze:
    scruffy,
        thin. In

the Museum of Modern Art
    head
        down, neck long as sadness

lowering to hanging ears
    (he's eyeless)
        that hear

nothing, and the sausage
    muzzle
        that leads him as

surely as eyes:
    he might
        be

dead, dried webs or clots of flesh
    and fur
        on the thin, long bones—but

isn't, obviously,
    is obviously
        traveling intent on his.

own aim: legs
　　　lofting
　　　　　with a gayety the dead aren't known

for. Going
　　　onward in one place,
　　　　　he doesn't so much ignore

as not recognize
　　　the well-
　　　　　dressed Sunday hun-

dreds who passing, pausing make
　　　his bronze
　　　　　road

move. Why
　　　do they come to admire
　　　　　him,

who wouldn't care for real dogs
　　　less raggy
　　　　　than he

is? It's his tragic
　　　insouciance
　　　　　bugs them? or is

it that art can make us
　　　cherish
　　　　　anything—this command

of shaping and abutting space—
    that makes us love
        even mutts,

even the world, having
    rocks
        and the wind for comrades?

It's not this starved hound,
    but Giacometti seeing
        him we see.

We'll stand in line all day
    to see one man
        love anything enough.

Ungainly Things

A regular country toad—pebbly,
    squat,
        shadow-green

as the shade of the spruces
    in the garden
        he came from—rode

to Paris in a hatbox
    to Lautrec's
        studio (skylights

on the skies of Paris)
    and stared
        from searchlight eyes,

dim yellow; bow-armed,
    ate
        cutworms from a box,

hopped
    occasionally
        among the furniture and easels,

while the clumsy little painter
    studied
        him in charcoal

until he was beautiful.
    One day
        he found his way

down stairs toward the world
    again,
        into the streets of Montmartre,

and, missing him, the painter-dwarf
    followed,
        peering among cobbles,

laughed at, searching
    until long past dark
        the length of the Avenue Frochot,

over and over,
    for the fisted, marble-eyed
        fellow

no one would ever see again
    except
        in sketches that make ungainly things beautiful.

Between Equals

A dragonfly blue as the June Atlantic
slim as its horizon
came over the dunes:

helicoptering off and on
a grass beside my chair,
not demanding money, nor love.

Nor did I want anything (money, love).
A small event.
He stayed. And went.

Ballad of the Mouse

A mouse the trap had slapped on, but not caught,
stood in the floor—
bloody whiskered—in the curious light
snapped on from the kitchen door:

grooved in the gray skull-fur
where the steel spring banged him,
blood from his ears, and one of two bead-black eyes
popped almost out, and hanging,

looking his bad luck, he skeered through doors,
rooms, halls, waddled along walls,
was exposed behind dressers,
hobbling with the load of his pain through falls,

bumps, skids, until the portable (peaches
can) prison (from the trash sack) fell
into place, changing the hellishly lighted chambers
to a pleasurably blackened cell

as comfortable as his hole, but showing
a scar of light around the rim.
A shirt cardboard slid under—moving floor—
and gathered him

into the lurch and claw-slipping tilt and
ride of air, and bore
him giddy, sloping and scratching
out the back door

to the yellow-porch-lit and midnight lawn,
and slid free his small terror
into the matty, spiny grass that held him like rails.
Shadowy, his executioner,

choosing (over drowning or crushing)
the doubtful love of a gun,
loomed over him, unready, tall. Unsteadily
he tried to run and the world blurred, un-

til he sat gathering his shakes in the grass-blades.
The long-barreled (.22, target) revolver lowered
to arm's length
toward the panting, furred bird-ribs not yet dead,

and aimed, and fired.
Six irregular shots
drove deep their thunderous metal seeds
flashing into the earth in spots

all around the tiny breath
they were meant for, spurting up yellow-brown
fountains of dirt
as before some palace, circus: forest, pillars, a kind of crown

in the noise and light of the murdering storm.
That poor marksman, love,
clicked, quietly
ticked, reloading, far, far, far above

the withered and dumb and dirt-daubled mouse.
Then light and leaden rain

stomped down again; and one blind iron tear
flooded all the sap of his pain

into the earth along with it, leaving—
indistinguishable in the churned-up lawn—
a flattened and sucked-out pelt
of half-buried once-mouse, now mouse-gone.

In the yellow-gloomed arena, death's main drag, beyond
which stars still leaked
the light of heaven onto woods
and hills the echoes had crashed and streaked

and rolled across from farm to farm,
in the ochre fungus of death, gun-handed, stone,
stood the hunter, victor—
tall, furious, foolish; alone.

Parable for Governors

In 1520
the Italians,
            in a formal court,
tried the field mice around Stelvio
        on charges of gravely damaging
                the crops.

Despite
a spirited
            defense, they were condemned
in absentia, and ordered to leave
        the countryside "within two weeks,"
                although

the old,
infirm, or very
                    young mice were (out of pity)
given twice as long. Farmers were urged
        to bridge their creeks
                for the exodus—

thus,
in the archives
                of the Court of Glorenza
in Val Venosta, near Bolanzo, the 2d of May;
        where it is not told, however,
                whether they left.

1. The Jaguar

On the right-hand page, this jaguar
that's
not a car

has turned his back
on
a jackal and a rabbit (jack)

(both quite scary-solemn)
in
the left-hand page's left-hand column.

The doe-eared jackal looks up,
and
the hare is ready to hop.

Clearly, plainly,
it
isn't their knowing merely, mainly,

that he'll eat them if he can
(being,
after all, no vegetarian)

that makes them so very, very glum,
but
that they'll have to come—

as the pages close—
right
under his nose!

2. The Armadillo

This scurrying pine cone of a fellow has an outside all leather-shingle and -quilt and -scale
from snout
to tail.

It probably is, however, more his habitat
than any
churlish habit that
makes him so much harder and homelier than many.

Small wonder he goes
nosing along with his roof and his bed on,
and tiptoes,
between Armada (Spanish, 1588) and Armageddon.

What Music Says

Tom the tom glides on grass on feet as smooth
as wheels; flows under a cliff of hedge
on axled shoulders, hunting
—a stub-tail, scruffy ex-killer, black and white
as if in bars.
               Wherever he goes, he's
prisoner of his own nature—
                       for Heckle and Jekyll,
two grackles, twin traveling jailors, bounce
on twigs, on wires, clucking steady warnings
at his journey
             (long tails tucking
at their trumpets' force)
                 and swoop overhead
to the next lawn.
          He'll eat neither bird,
squirrel, chipmunk, nor mouse,
nor anyone whose ears are to a tune.

Seal on an Island-Rock

A part of rock—yards up from the surf's white
churn—proved smoother than a rock,
wetter, tilting out toward the horizon a muzzle
like a pirate twenty-pounder

(same profile, heavy in haunch)
and turned to us on the sand-rock beach its
eyes, thin drooping whiskers, and comedian's
pause till the house has quieted.

He shook then, doggily, and set his gaze
back on the sea, honked out a warning
or a love cry to whatever might
be down there, in or on or beyond its green,

and balancing, flippering with a perfect
Chaplin clumsiness, trundled forward
to the edge of rock and, flapping,
clapped himself down his private avalanche

into the slithering waves; and then enacted
something swimming, floating, blowing
noseholes at the sky. Commotion
that might have emptied the sea of fish!

Not half a mile from Gay Head Light, he swirled
along; and hid; and brought his rainstorm
dripping up on the rock's low slope,
shook, galumphed *urf-urfing* to his perch again.

One of our kind, doing it by rote for praise,
all afternoon he struggled,
swam, itched, sang, dove, lovingly
for tourists, for pictures, and for poems.

The Turtle

Put in my rooms for a joke,
    this fellow—
                      pudgy in reptilian skin,
dried, shaggy folds on (wee elephant-tailed)
rump,
        on jowls,
and on his huge, nailed paddle legs—
clunks and bumps along the walls,
                         tipping
up over a lamp base, books; breast-
stroking his ungainly way
in the strange, dry element,
                    plodding,
swimming with strong, clawed, backward
strokes toward water,
                  neck out, dots and parallel
swervy lines of dusty black extending
to wide eyes, the cigar-clipper snout
    (breath holes),
a cable neck drawing his heavy
banging house onward to his watery
                        will.
Picked up,
        he can hardly close
his battered plates; the head,
                withdrawn
into its penis-hide, slowly
stretching its fold of mantle with it, sticks back out,
    retreats

at every nudge or tilt in the unfamiliar,
eye-level
      air;
          pushes out again.
Hissing and lunging at the dogs,
who sniff him,
          he will not back up. Snaps.
Let be, he rattles through his circuit
of walls,
      over and over,
          an archaic tank
(plated, cannon-necked) thumping baseboards
to define a place one can be in
but cannot go from—
         until
I take him to the dock,
         air, salt, and flies.
   In sweeping (scratchy) strides
across the weathered boards he throws himself,
sure of direction,
        exonerated,
into the inlet's splashy, deep, green racing-past.

From Across the Bay

Egrets, icy on storm-ink blue
that darkens lightly every instant,
thread homeward, flapping, in straggling lines,
in bunches. They are as startling white

as the waves the wind lips on the bay's
black-green toward us, their great wings leafing
air as they come long-leggedly dropping
into the pale salt marsh's tufty

windrow cedars, to sit like candles
on the storm's limbs, white, wind-fluttered.
The rain when it comes will drench them,
the dark pinch them out, as it batters

and wrestles runneling at our windows.
Clearings hacked by lightning will show
them—wet, white half seconds—still there:
asleep, waiting, a kind of certainty.

Post-Watching: Little Night Heron

The summer nearly over, here,
   and running down like a clock,
we watch a young night heron maneuver
   on an abandoned dock

at sunset, with the madras light
   behind him on the marsh.
His eye, sparky in the west-glow,
   is glassy-orange, and harsh.

Wind from the sea frills out his feathers,
   ruffs his hump-necked crown.
He hunches there in leaden shoulders,
   suspicious, speckly brown;

his long thin legs (and splayed-wire toes)
   seem dusted with blue-lime sheen,
as does the long, deep beak he uses,
   stretching his neck up, to preen

occasionally beneath his wings.
   Itch. Itch. The sun goes down,
sinks farther south, day after day,
   colder, redder, round.

The distant cedars have filled by now
   with egrets, white as snow,
pale sleeping flags. But this one querulous
   heron wants to know

what all the changes are about
   as the sky, and year, go dim.
Summer is gone. Somebody's going
   to have to explain to him.

Fly in December

In an old, dark house—
where the thick light held us
bowled in glass—

looping from nowhere, furious, he came
pirouetting, hurling
a black, drunken aim,

zanging, unzipping the halves of the air
all afternoon and evening,
singing black in eye and ear

at the dog, at me, at the light,
flinging,
bitter, rude, a piece of night,

or, overhead, rode invisibly
in the terrier's shouldered, worried glance
on some vague journey

through doors into the other rooms,
back, wrestling
whatever angel he held, or doom:

death, the sweetness gone, the loss of summer.
At midnight, he stopped
suddenly, letting the windows remember

the late snow falling to and fro
again, the furry
stars that burn in lovely agonies as they go

beyond our tiny night.
Vile
star—breath—flower!—knot

that won't pull loose to dying,
does he see
at last what is always too late for deriding,

perched somewhere, dumb,
watching in a hundred eyes or—blind?—
having let it come?

Whatever.
          In the old, dark house
we have settled down for the night,
somehow, the three of us.

Birds and the Moonlight

The moon's fake daylight wakes the birds.
Their scratchy cries and murderous dreams
keep me awake; and I go out
among them, as if to give them what for.

Trees and their shadows are equal dark,
a web of sticks, a thicket tangling
dim earth and air; and the moon's ice,
silvering on the roof, skates angels.

Poor creatures cannot sleep, by God!

These shadowy roots hunched in the air
have fish in them, light, iron minnows
that dart in time like swift reflections
of the stars.
                        Some entry has been forced.

The waterless birds of day sing blind
in this dawn that never yellows into flowers,
letting the shadows free, that stays
like after the world has begun to end.

Mammoth's Journey

Across an Arctic bay,
    the bluff of a glacier, white, tall,
crumbling, a frozen river
tumbling eons out of the mountains,
    cracking, melting
into the sun, into a summer sea.
Ice-bits on cold green sparkle;
                  white
pygmy whales sport in the breakers.

River of beasts, studded with their bones!

There: in the very act of shattering
the icy crypt,
        breaking out of a twisting
hundred-century tunnel in the dark—
enormous,
        tusks curling up like hooks
or arms bent up to carry grief forever,
    going into the air;
the huge, half-fleshy skull gazing darkly,
    domed, emaciated
in the sunlight,
ice water trickling from its open jaws;
    a poised stump of foreleg
extending, cautiously,
          for a next foothold

which has already fallen, or runneled
away;
        a dancer at the curtain—

      Mammoth! skeleton!
                 shards
of hide, rust-colored wool, great handfuls
    of dark hair long
and loose as the hairs of a horse's tail

: a drunkard's dream,

half-rotted, hairy, huge, emerging dimly
from a wall of ice, stinking,
                stepping
outward into air,
           great shaggy bones
still holding the shape of flood
or avalanche like a dream about them,
                    bones
jostled into myopic disarray,
             bones
wading toward the sea,
          the plunge, the lacy,
   glittering waves.

2

In the Leaves of Time

1   Man was not man, and will not be:
in the sky, a book turned open to the night,
the stars that hung like shaking light-year petals
      to our cold amphibian eye,
on that first shore,
      have drifted in the winds of nothingness,
changed, stretched, gone out,
their messages of light illegible, a script
      refreshed in blossoming fire
from beyond time's edge—the pages
      bright, undecipherable,
gazed at by the faceless men, halfmen, not men,
      lusting, staring upward,
      at the windows of the dream.

The dinosaurs are blown (light
as leaves) across the floors of time;
mountains on a summer's day, ephemerae,
    swarm
where "waterdrops have worn the stones
and blind oblivion swallowed cities up."
No leaf remains that fluttered to the tunes
      of far, archaic springs;
rock pushes up, dissolves, and pushes up,
its tiny-ribbed lockets of the past,
      skeletal hieroglyphics,
grind in the earth, wear in the sea's deep winds.

Only light, unchanged, flows in our eyes
as in the trilobite's lost, sandy gaze
        at the mysterious text—

        the changing dance of things,
        of life, of worlds:
"the singing reptile in the bird."

2   Sweet earth! sweet ancient earth, once
            eye of space,
now merely another glittering among the glitterings
that plumb our unfathomable everywhere!
        Stars perish,
leaves; men perish, races of men
    —those halfmen, brothers, huge-browed,
shoulders to the sky,
                    whose tracks fade
pastwards into the darkling leaves and tangles
        of earths we could not comprehend,
the original twilit planet of the beast,
        legends told in bones.

Hardly men—faces of a nightmare?
        in Europe, Asia, Africa,
a myriad dream, recurring, beginning,
        eyes: eyes
that look toward us, staring, but do not see
        even our shapes
beyond the mists and glacier-turning boulders:

true Prometheus, dark, hairy by a fire;
slender apes,
                lofting through trees like spiders
in a web of branches,
                        who somehow, unaccountably,
dream of tools in fetid nights;
gorilloid faces, shapes,
                        the hunky brows: eyes,
when Europe like a mirror took the ice
        and mammoths lurched
their hairy caravans among the sounds of falling
rock and snow,
                of groaning mountains,
of winter hung year round upon a ghostly land
        of bitter winds and smoky caves
and tiny figures—see them!—hurrying
in a dusk of avalanches:
                        a world clouded in ice,
        wide, creaking silences,
stone-bearing rivers of the white forever,
cities . . . buried in the future of the landscape
        like laddered, spidery jewels
time would expose, beneath the heavy tread
        we recognize:

                men; man;

on the ridges of time, the sentimental brute,
the beast that recognizes death,

that dreams hereafters,
the animal that kills its kind,
the monster grasping a stone or the energies of the sun
who grieves, who buries his dead with love,
trinkets—flints, berries, colored stones—
        for the journey all dead make.
We come upon the signals of the grave,

                        illegible,

        dark caves in the chasm
of the Neander, by La Chapelle-aux-Saints,
        the message of the dawn:
*We also were men, knew pain, feared, loved, dreamed
        journeys beyond the moon
and clouds; perished like leaves beneath the wind.*

We turn the pages of their dust
—sorrows that have no country, struggling
        between mud and heaven—
and read our restless quests, all our deaths,
our prayers and telescopes like guns and faces
        lifted, searching
darkness for the villages among the stars.

3   The other,
                and ourselves!
                        Time's torrent
sweeps dark and turbid, unbroken,
impetuous, toward the sea from which rose
once our salty blood, our calciferous bones,
        from which the grasses marched up,

and trees, crabs, ants, birds, and the many eyes
       that look out at us
from the leaves, follow from hidings in the forest
       our mysterious steps among them:
tiny eyes in faces strangely like ours, turned
       miming toward us . . .
                              that seem our own!

    Many, the one!

Walking these ancient, cloudy landscapes
       where ice-heaved boulders
tumble like gravestones, where gods never were,
       these terrible barrens
where man was born into the wind and hawks
       (black rips in heaven) drift
still across the shifting centuries and suns,
it is not despair we feel on desolate slopes,
       but freedom, the grandeur
of the myriad and ever-unfolding thing we are.
As granite as the stone that grinds us,
       as much the wind
as the wind that swirls about our heads:

    we confront ourselves:

the amorous, illimitable blood,
the crazy seeds bursting upwards in a dark
through which walls crumble and pediments' golden
       truths
like rocks in the sea sink into vines and ageless earth.
We are the enduring green for which the sickle comes,

the eyes among its leaves,
the sky beyond in mineral bud and flower!

If one by one the races change, drift, die,
    yet forms, and forms of the forms
across epochs—phyla, those finer beasts—
re-emerge upon the misty spaces,
                        the fields of ice,
the brilliant meadows of the fire.
We are the diamond in the leaves of time,
which, helpless, singing, can only flow
and chant about us, round, and round, and round;
we are the faceless, nameless greater creature
    with many faces, many names,
the marvelous, deeper animal we see look back
from the brown, sweet eyes of dogs,
the lion's glance,
                        the lemur's almost human gaze,
the bird's black flash and the lizard's bead.
Behind us, ourselves peer out at the changing sky,
    unchanging light.
Our hands are not the only hands
    that grasp a bough
or tear the fruit off of the hunger of the sun.
The unceasing root, though limbs dry, perish, rot,
sends branchings green and tall into the sky.

We need fear nothing, not even ourselves
    (our insane fist, or bombs)
: on our most distant, final day, somewhere,
    hidden in leaves or tall grass
    or in the moony dark,

the greater creature whom we are
will stroke its young with other hands,
speak with the noise before words,

                    be warm in fur

    or safe again in scales
beneath the waters' pluck and strumming;
will love, suffer, sleep into the dawn
that only, ever, forever, comes.
Somewhere, even in that last, man's farthest hour
    when the moon puts on its petals,
    the creature we are,
a creature with hands like ours,

              and eyes,
will be already dreaming of beginning again
upon the road that leads among the stars,

in that sleepless breeze,

           dreaming, dreaming:
  . . . of beginning again.

3

Lines for a Discouraged Friend Digging
in His Garden

I'm here in admiration.
Hoe and spade,
seed, sprout, and flower,
the vegetable rows,
are every bit as good, as fine
as the versing trade;
the finished garden,
real in time,
immortal as a poem.

And very like! Both
deal in rows,
or lines, take labor
and common luck,
need tending carefully,
but do not keep
a family
or save the soul.

Quick as overnight in poems,
in the strings
and sticks of stanzas,
the humdrum
words leaf out like lettuces,
faults in as green
profusion, as random, bright,
as weeds. Dark,
caterpillar noises

chew ruin along the silence;
syllables flutter upward
like beans toward
the clouds . . . or, heavy,
like potatoes grow
and bulge beneath
the rows, sending out a dusty
music as their leaves.

I play—but play at truth,
for the feeling's true.
No words can pull
that carrot
up, earth clinging
to its colors, perfect
in the burning sun.
You err to doubt?
The art, perhaps,
is to see the art?
I'm serious now.
The order that we find
or order that we make
of what we find:
man's part in nature's,
poem or garden—
both are works of mind.
A garden is
its own fine pastoral—
don't pale orange, hairy
squash-blooms or flower-plots
shame sonnets, more than not?
I envy, willingly,

your shining labor
published
in the burning sun.

And it is nothing
that they are, both,
less beautiful
than what we had pursued
from catalog
or winter midnight's dream;
poems, imperfect,
fail as gardens do.
Death's weather spoiling
blossoms, harvests
poems equally?
Where's your argument?
Poems fade, go
out of style, are dumb—
how many molder
finally back
into roots and flowers
as the dreadful years pass on?
All grasses over
in the fall
of year, of time, of man.

Poets and gardeners—
tiny figures
in the sun, muttering
lines that won't come right
or bringing water
in buckets from the tap—

we prune and trim,
we delve or hoe
and struggle
to make the plants,
or poems, grow.
And it is less than nothing
that gardens fade,
or poems crumble
in November, into darks,
the pageless earth.
Love, in any case,
is what we raise—
and order, won
from the wilderness of world
and year.
Love, and *Order*—
and that they perish
became our season,
the tools from other hands,
the one unreasoning reason
for the spirit's joy
in toiling rhyme or soil.
In friendliness to his sons
good Adam died.

In time time gets both . . .
the murals at Pompeii,
fountains of Alhambra,
bright green groves
Epicurus kept,
the villa grounds at Palmieri,
Alcinous' gardens

Homer told of,
Babylon, old Eden,
Virgil, Marvell, Pope,
poem and garden,
poet, gardener, all.

All-getting,
all-begetting time—
only our sweetest enemy
and friend, all-
making, -breaking time—
only turns the pages
we write on, the furrows
from which the spirit's green
sprouts up again.
Even the sun will stay
at last,
the flowering sun,
to say all poems'
and all gardens' praise.

An Epitaph

He recorded the world in words
for years: the blue, green, brown;
all faces, days, tides, birds.
Now he takes the silence down.

The Poets

Tongues laden with the sweet, slow
syllables,
bronze, gold, round, leaden, they

come unlovely, pompous, made drunk
out of their minds,
sly, and touching girls. Fat clings

like buttresses upon their ribs.
Their musc,
death, webs their tolling eyes,

their breaths. Singers, singing, they
stumble, climbing,
talking, old mouthfuls of bells.

Fable

The poets stopped. One dawn or another none of them
wrote anymore;
afterwards, it seemed to have been that simple.

They couldn't explain. Months passed or maybe years, slow
rumors spread;
someone thought they might have stopped forever.

Critics, the last of all to notice, complained.
A Senator spoke
for the record. Letters to the Editor followed, forums,

handsome offers. The President urged resumption of "this
magnificent
public service." The Dow-Jones slid a fraction.

But they were gone, as down in darkling green
crabs sink sideways
past light, or as a butterfly closes his wings

upon a fence wire in the frostiness of October.
No one who could say
truly what such a loss might mean came forward.

Nothing in fact seemed to change. Days still were days;
moon, stars went along
shining as before. Lovers loved. Heroes had wars.

The small birds vanished and returned, sang;
schoolyards lay dusty
in August sun. The world went on in smoking rains,

in red and glass-gold weathers, in snowy mornings
when the butterflies
were dead and sticks walked upright on the rivers.

First Snow

I sit at my desk in the dawning;
a gray light—
        the first snow
moves, neither rising nor falling,
motes, a dry pollen, riding
a wind that is hardly a wind.

I know the terrible flower that comes
of it—
     and shall sleep, anyhow,
while it happens, knowing twilight
will have me going my three
miles booting in its fallen petals.

For the Season

On a wintry parkway, far and deep
in black Connecticut,
we crested
on a lit Christmas tree of cars:
red,
slender,
blinking, tall
as something, Danish,
rising to the next long wooded ridge,
topped with real stars.

Dark snow on either side, outbuildings, woods,
dark farms,
the countryside itself
a sky of occasional, furry lights,
and rabbits in cold leaves.

We rode that tree, right up its lights!

Among the Piles of Street-Light

Nights, the snowplow shakes
windows along the street.
Even the roar frightens the mothy
snow, which beats against the panes.
Lights: a red eye turning, a blue
eye flashing, head-eyes, and eyes
that light its lumbering, long,
arched, grinding thorax: a girder-
mantis amid its yellow limbs,
tunneling in the falling snow
beneath a web of leafless branches.
On huge black paws, like boots,
it turns, resumes; a single
silver mandible chews out white.
Roughly trundling, bright, wildly
blinking, it passes again among
the cocooned hulks of cars, piling
up the street-light, and the moths.

In Winter

It is hard, inland,
        in winter,
when the fields are motionless in snow,

to remember waves, to remember
        the wide, sloshing
immensity

of the Atlantic, continuous,
        green in the cold, taking snow
or rain into itself,

to realize the endurance
        of the tilting bell buoy
(hour by hour, years

through) that clangs, clangs,
        leaning
with the rocking waters, miles

from land; even in storm and
        night-howling
snow, wet, red, flashing

to mark the channel. Some
        things
are, even if no one comes.

The January Sky Is Blue and Cold

By the snowy curb
    a tossed
        out tree, sans lights

or star or baubles,
    lies,
        rolls, rolls a little

in the bitter wind—tinsels
    aleap.
        Strands

shimmering loose, day-stars,
    air, caught,
        rise, flash past roofs, away,

as sun on water shivers.
    There's always more
        to anything,

it seems. The white,
    city garbage truck heaves
        off, bedecked

with greens, a woods, birds,
    feathers, onward, a vessel
        of love. Tiny

fires will flicker up
    for mowers, silver
        in green, come May!

Cape Cod in March

Only the sea looks like summer.
It rollicks its leafy waves,
and turns them. The light
is thin; and the air, chill,
blows too keenly for standing
on the shore, on the windy dunes.
The houses, shuttered, huddled
upon the winter-colored downs,
still cower like silly creatures
who still expect a misfortune
they don't know now won't come.
Everywhere, the dry salt grass
rustles; and the sky, sunny,
pewter, changes as no summer
changes its skies. But the towns
liven. White is being painted
whiter, and people have begun
to move about; the trees along
the little streets are swarmed
with buds, green, scarlet, gray.
In a week or two, forsythia
will shower its peaceful rockets
all over the towns. Meanwhile,
the arm of land lets out
its tiny fleets, trying riggings,
turning the wintry sea
toy-size again. And if gulls
like ancient snow ride motionless

on channels, creeks, edges
of things, robins have come
without persuasion, like
burghers, for the coins of spring.

In the Field Forever

Sun's a roaring dandelion, hour by hour.
Sometimes the moon's a scythe, sometimes a silver flower.
But the stars! all night long the stars are clover,
Over, and over, and over!

Out for Stars

We walked out late, leaning back for stars
beneath the staked-down tent of dark,
gawking there like foreigners
at high, and myriad, and stark,

until we turned tired from them, stiff-
eyed with staying for a meteor's track,
and saw below, in the tide-creek's slough,
faint bits of glassy fire in the black

that flowed around the pilings: glowed,
and faded, and glowed again. Deep in,
haze-firefly green; and where it rode
the crinkling surface, pale blue winks

and sparks. A long-handled net we swished
them with, they made burn all blue-white
as if electrified. We fished
some up—clear jelly in a match-light,

but in the dark striped, icy fire
the net strained out, let slide through, plop
and glowing back into the choir.
Soft stars! that let us take them up.

Morning at Menemsha

A fly, summering all morning on Martha's Vineyard,
has a frenzy. Zzz-zzz-zzz in the air,
while the bell-buoy bell is donging
some hour or wave or minuteness everywhere.
Nothing that's said or done can be changed.

The writer writing in his little house
away from the house sees none of the children,
or the gulls, or the robin whose front
is August-burned as pale as the grass-ends.
Nothing that's said or done can be changed.

The ten-inch snake under the beach bush
winds his neck back, slides off ready to put
teeth into a finger. None of us can remember
whether he was white on brown or brown on white.
Nothing that's said or done can be changed.

Scrub pine, pin oaks, things sea-gnarled or rough;
the porch's white rail and Buzzard's Bay behind,
and a view all the way to a sun so bluely
heavened, we might all be angels if we climbed.
Nothing that's said or done can be changed.

Climbing at Gay Head

Not as young as the children,
we all threw sea-carved rocks
at sea-carved rocks thrown
up for targets, and missed (a
field of sky-rock fire perilous
to gulls); and not as young
as the children, we heaved stones
at surf-brimmed boulders farther
out (hats on deep, sea-thrusting
titan-walkers), enjoying the tall
ponk-splashes, the occasional
hit-*tunk*-and-horizonward
ricochet. We went along
the beach like plunderers, wet
trousered, spreading, turning
boards: men, wives, lovers,
and the dwarf army of their kids
in front, hallooing. At the cliffs
(which wear askew a lighthouse
like a party hat) we all scrambled
up the not-quite-too-steep,
eroded, sand-clay face, balancing
on loosing grains, or air,
slipping, making fingers do
things in water fissures,
until, three-quarters up,
looking down at the rock-
scarred beach, or outward to
the tipping sea-horizon,

we faltered, spread as hawks on wind,
and, not as young as the children,
knew we were too high,
and clutched, slid, clung, grabbed
stub-end dust-pull rootlets,
grappling with prehensile knees
toward the dusty, overhanging
green's coverlet: where, knowing
fiercely, yearning for an underfoot
(not used to so much overhead), we
took gladly the strong, wax-
red-green wreaths of poison ivy
in reaching handfuls, to pull
up onto, into a field of it.
Not as young as the children,
the sky around our shoulders
like an arm, we carried home
bent toes, sliced fingers, knees, clay-
tangled hair, pulled elbows, and
a vision as from Eden's top
of the descending generations
small upon the slopes of time.

After the Swimmer

Clear, the shaken water
busies in its claws
clouds, light,
from which he climbed.

For Cass
                        May 1966

How does one wish well
a child, born in a year
of war and flickering
outrage beyond any
window one looks from?
Trees rustle thinly,
old tall feathered heads,
in the migraine air.
A May with snow, cloudy,
the poisoned sparrows
and last year's last
leaves bouncing on limb
and limb. Cars stream
past, a ribboning haze
as if in glass, the cords
tightening in sun,
strangling, colored, bright.
Little model trees,
like demons, wave their sleeves.
At the end of the block
another woods goes down,
jumbled by steel jaws;
the blue jays will move.
Whole forests fall
somewhere, flow
splintering to our doors:
crashes; the Indian
floods; queens; beatings;

brown hatred in the streets;
napalm on towns,
on mountains; politicians'
mealy absurdities.
"More war is peace."
Villages burn in clearings,
on TV;
children—black, weeping
terrorists—huddle
before the guns. *Relief
of minor headache pain.*
Earth's troubles reach
out, blinkings, insensate,
before the late-
late show. Within that eye
our deaths like webs
blossom orangeish green
and—as the real night turns
and we sleep—blur,
deepen, and constrict.
In the long, star-wheeling
darks, somewhere,
unholy in the gloom and brush,
unbidden, the Republic
founders.

      A child?
to celebrate a child?
Yet, yes, the green breaks
through—up, out,
bursts overhead in dawns
that hear (not groaning

trailers on Truck Hill,
but) avalanching codes
of light the far, windy
sun spends
into its everywhere.
Graves climb the hill.
The world is real.
In noon, the dogwoods
in a half-ruined woods make
butterflies . . . trembling
lamps, swarms, leafy stars.
Petals drift off, wing,
and fall. The workmen
resume, clatter: shards
of yellow, metal teeth chomping
at the green that hides
machines.

       Noons fall.

           Words?
words to celebrate a child?
to answer the hurt
of a mother's
flesh, the torn placenta,
death like a hole
life climbs darkly out of?
Even the room, harbor
of spikes and flowers,
pales with the pain,
the vanishing loveliness
of a girl, a hardening

of death into bones
that cannot smile enough,
a father's all-weathering
joy.

　　Noon falls.

How praise that child?
old, wizened, selfish—
the father of its parents'
pain, their patriarch
of an unending dust, of time.
Unending? all one
man sees from the hill
of his days, the simple
valley, woods, and village—
beyond which the world
lies, always, journeys
no man can ever take.
The world is not enough:
the birds, the blue jays,
dancing sparrows on a bough.
Nights wheel above our heads;
starry-fixed, unreal.
Is love pain's flower?
our dying's only gift?
Is love the single affirmation,
as the ticking hours
of afternoon bend in, on,
toward their end, as
(ever unfinished)
the flowers have their pain,

more beautiful than love?
Is love all?

       All!
I cannot speak—child,
alight with pain
as swift gold—
until it is too late
to understand, upon the tree,
or from the sandy rock
that grows in geometrical
blooms where green was,
or in the eyes of old-men children
in jungles no farther
than my hand, or out past stars,
how, to the dead
and the unborn—radiant
in the sunlight—pain makes
us, murdering,
like petals on a tree.

4

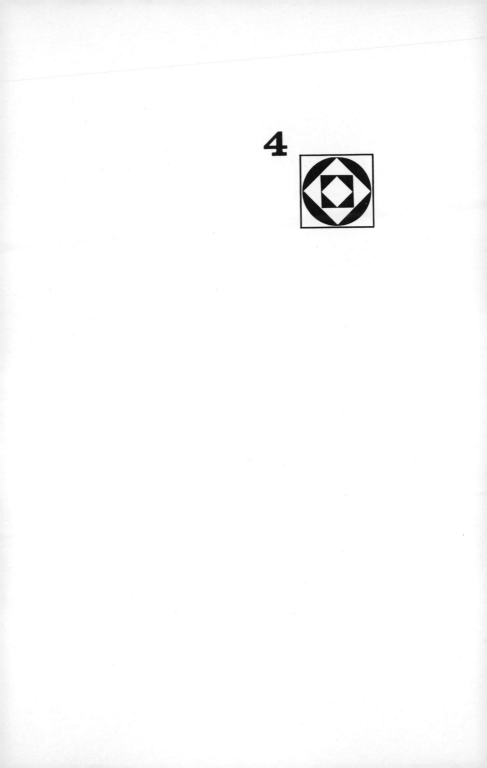

Susan

1   Starting with nothing—
                     "Look. There's a Catskill."
A cloud.
          The torn pines along the rocks—
slaty bluff fallen into the river's edge,
vertical, tilted,
                like a graveyard to its eyes
in sand—
"Say, whatever became of the mountains?"
         —in history: torn pines,
                    a dreaming.
Dusks on the Hudson,
             rocks; the glassy water
sucks away from the rocks as the current
slides toward New York,
            little backward waves
sucking in the dark.
The city will be there.
Lyn! "It is a mountain." O Ed!
Sucking.
        —Nothing. Love.

2   But the barges came,
            lights, like acolytes,
moving on the moving waters; slowly; working
down from Albany. Only the lights.
The tug is a party of lights, red, white,
high; shining windows; masted
            —" . . . live on them"—

slowly, carrying what out of what mountains
we cannot see?
               and the barge lights,
dim, brownish, open lights in the river air,
—a train of them, steady,
                      like candles,
seen through the torn pines. As broken
ice passed, weeks ago, shuffling,
behind the pines.

3   —damned window was
blue again!
          —high, small, and blue—
shimmering as the water surface of a well
to which he looks up; from the shadowy
drownings.
         Nothing.
Trees, mornings, birds!
                Who was betrayed?
         —easier than to climb up toward it.
The ropes of blood, from what are they hung?
and the ledges of bone?
                 —until the spirit
can look out of eyes, and glass, and sky.
Out of her!
Oh, we'll dance, dance,
dance on our comfortable deaths,
singing upon the sill
                —dreamings.
The city: love in how many windows?
only the elevator lights.
           Drownings.

4 The candle, in a clear bottle, the wooden table,
blinks:
   wind: a curve of ragged blue—
the edge of pennants! blue as the morning!—
flutters from the wick.
     A hand.
"One of the Queens went up to Albany once."
Flames.
   —up past the rocks,
       a shapely palace
glittering between the darkened hills.
Flutters blue.
   Wind: he wonders,
watching the barges drawing even,
lights of houses on the other shore
       gathering
to watch:
   "Was it a Queen?"
—and shall a girl love this man,
his mornings?

5 Wind. Wind. Sets.
marching the long forests of the sea . . .
flutters.
   —love him?
      . . . unbuttoning?
Earlier, the day was clouding over,
the sun, breaking, made a light
like golden foil on the waters,
      moving:
the green pines. And, later, it will rain:
elsewhere, so

he'll notice the pavement is wet
in the headlights, but not here
: candles, barges.
>The dry pines; the bluff
behind them, rocks, still leafless trees,
sun shining on the waters.
>He found,
in a rock crack—a foot from the waters—
tiny white flowers, a nest of wiry stems, green,
spiky,
>stars: and picked one.

6   The forests of the sea can't be deciduous,
hiding bones—
>" . . . a Catskill"
—to which the waters roll.
>Twilight.
Dark.
>Dreaming: sideways,
>teeth;
skull to skull,
>sucking; and her fine hair
in which he drowns, sweet weeds, roiling,
green, over him; dark,
>the tent of her face;
her hair: falling: and dies
in the shade of her mouth.
>Leafy!
Flows . . .
>—little backward waves,
barge lights. Wind.
Children, all sorts of children, he thinks,

will be playing
in the cemetery's watery

               green edge
: glass walls, gardens, sunny,
blooming with fish and bones.

                    —love him?

7   —blinks.
Cool.
          . . . flutters. In dark, upriver, searchlights
find the clouds and swim across them,
round, round, the gray lights turning crumpled along
the shapeless roof.

              By the river. Trees.
—oils of her love.

              —dark. And, every morning,
the scent of sheets, clean, like flowers,
and the window

              —small, high—
the fresh scent of her cotton shirt, her

                    ears
: the clean skull loving him. Watching her?
He dreams.

              —toward the necklace of the bridge,
high, in the night, far
below where they are. Even the waters
are moving:

             shapes of fruits dangling
in the shadowy leaves,

               toward which he goes.

8   Nothing? Love?
                    "... and peed into the river
from a bluff up there" (pointing)
 : in the candlelight, above a clear bottle ...
the torn trees, ice moving,
herds, crunching
                 —toward the deathless sea.
 : a shining arc.
He threw the flower onto the river,
its only star,
             cargo drifting ...
bouncing with straw, logs, on the water slick
with faint light,
               hours into the dark
or in the dawning, by piers,
a gift
         —passing the city toward the sea.

9   In the leaves of her, clear,
                  her love—
lighted, like a park path at midnight, drifted
loose with its trees and floating past
the rocks down toward the bridge
                  —acolytes?
and shrubs, sailing.
Imagines: her reading, in a lighted window,
clean above the trees.
Below, below the bridge,
                the miles of night flow
outward: the brown lights vanishing
after them.
           Bank lights stay.

                    You two—
    Ed, Lynie!
                Searchlights prowl. Prowl.
    Torn pines were green that now are dark—
    after them

10   : car windows open, after rain
    —"Rained. The streets are wet."—
    wind in the windows, headlights,
                                the curving road
    up among darks, among trees on either side
    hurting to grow leaves from their fingers:
    —love him?
                    Stoplights: in the wet air:
    blooming red and green, and
                                —toward a spring night—
    open windows:
                    a star, straw, bouncing onward
    between the dark shores;

        streetlamps, leafy: her.

5

Moving

Bookshelves empty, tables lampless, walls
bare, the house is a rubble of moving—
foothills of boxes, trunks
under clouds of ceiling.

Friends
said good-bye hours ago, when June twilight
hung on the hills. Now, in late dark too
muggy for stars, moths whir to the yellow porch-light,
ping screens. By the one dim floor lamp
among the shadowy undoings of my life,
in a limbo between having gone and having gone,
I sit like a caretaker of my doom.
Not an ashtray or a spoon.
In the real dawn, I will be going.

My friends, sleeping, turned toward
tomorrows without me, will still be dreaming
when I begin to drive the familiar streets and roads
into which the movers will come after me,
in which the flowering sun will come only after me.
If I called anyone now, in this steep hollow
past midnight, all I said would
be from the future.

Alone in the present,
I wait, smoking (a tin can for ashes).
Night like a heaven of little noises, snaps, sea-creaks, wingy
silences I'm voyaging through,

surrounds me. Beyond love
I am a projectile into the future—
still hours, days away.
Time has stopped at the speed I am going, landmarks
appear strangely in new light,
clouds whirling past me, into the past.

The phone has been disconnected.

A Testament

I am a sort of ark, lofting
blood, bone, eye,
love, hate, all mated contraries.
Time's the flood—

on the rafters of my skull
for forty summers and forty springs!
Even the splashing dreams
and doubts pulled

up from swimming have paired,
and settled down in dirty straw and families.
O sweet debris,
suppose the rain is everything, forever?

endurance the only love?
I am an ark, awash,
freighting whatever is, coasting
these glassy waters

whose only shore is down:
in the dim, cold shadows, silver, the lucky
ones
(unseen) nuzzling Ararat.

After Parting

Only your telephoned voice,
saying you are all right,
thin and awkward
at a distance,
a mechanical insect, comes

—like a sudden postcard,
still and colored, come upon
in an untidied drawer:

quick with reminding
of the sunned stones
and fountains of a square in the casual interior,
of the green mountains,
the bird-cliff walls of windows
in a foreign street,
of the presence,
of the forever being there.

The Body Waking

The dim, unpopulated islands of
true sleep,
my only kingdom, dissolve

into the circling sounds, the othering world.
The waters
waste—and deep inside my being, curled,

uncoiling to a light that burns
like ice-glow
bloody, gloomy through my caverns,

something dreadful, bestial, not-I, up toward time's
riot
and greening climbs

by ropes of blood, up ledges of bone
within me,
hauling: Oh, I am not my own,

struggling to struggle with what dies,
lurching
as it hoists itself within my eyes . . .

and sees its blond unshaven shadow
blink
back from the mirror's morning window.

The Saturday Morning of Lemuel Hill

The trucks at dawn grind their lights
beyond the grid of sleeping maples;
green is not green at dawn.

He turns. The shade is thin with light.
Angels of the ceiling drift
across his sight; the plaster leaves

settle where such powdery wings have flown.
Resist. The distant sputter of trucks
resumes. Resist. His dreamings fold

him into landscapes colored like the day,
but farther off, deeper—brighter—
where Alps, like sunrise sherberts, rise

in streams of morning liquors to his eyes.

For Lawson and Ann

White solidness of rooms;
simple, dark
colors of the furnishings, things,
carpets, lit

against blackness:
the bright,
stored rectangles of your lives.
Upstairs

the children sleep; outside
trees
sing to a June darkness.
Talking, I think

of death, and of hospitality
—how you, keeping
the world out,
go meaningfully into your years

in the long days and longer nights
when we,
wherever we are, can only
picture you here.

Love

Uncertain what love is,
even that it is,

he scorned the easy word,
fence-hearts,

film's end, the angry millions
professing

but still unhappy, drunk, mean,
dying, who etch

equations on rank walls—until
he came unwary

upon her lovely need: tears, hope.
Hers? His in her?

But question reaches to question,
and since, for the dying,

there never will be merely time,
he said the word;

and thought that love might be
as much as

(never knowing) to believe it is,
for someone else.

On the College Archery Range

Girls, at bows, string concentric blooms
on the distances of aim,
these leafy afternoons;
huntresses, in a game.

The arrows as often lodge in trees or grass
as in the rings. They practice
only grace
that pierces lovers—for the fact is

they are themselves (beautifully)
death's small deer.
The beauty is, how wholly
they attend their huntings here.

The Clarinet

Alone, up attic in the old steep house
—where, in trunks, pink silks, lace, button shoes
neatly folded, await the resurrection—
I found a clarinet I had forgotten;

and, after twenty years, my fingers
(or the memory of fingers, since the boy's hands
have been remattered more than twice since then)
still limberly remembered how to make

the silver keys tick on among themselves
like fine machines and make, in the shadowy light,
music rise out along a frosting breath.
It was a proof of spirit: those ghostly hands

round the dark tube, candled, tallowed in silver,
singing in an empty and night-fallen house
in winter. I hurled eighth notes at time,
"Blue Bells of Scotland" at the clinging cold,

roared "Annie Laurie" as if the dead danced, flung
a melody of Schumann's into the night
—no matter that the tones cracked, the reed screeked!
or that the tunes were silly. Their colored scraps

shook on the dark beyond blank windows, hung,
pennants of breath, bright, quick—answer
to the whole grim day, whose leaves like clouds of mice
raced in the road, and to the night's stone ear.

Little by Little

I move toward you by difficult halves,
like Xeno's dwindling steps that prove
mountains impossible,
and spring, and selves that can love.

Yet, opening, spring's illogic blurs
solipsisms of thrush and petal;
mountains nudge and nurse at the sky.
And I am coming—oh, little by little!

Aubade: N.Y.C.

it is morning darling look the sun
by the fire escape comes peeping
rose on our sheets how fresh how
still oh and the roaches are sleeping

Love Poem

It is our first Christmas, now,
And our first Christmas apart.
The long morning, without voices,
Grows stiff with snow. Spruces

Huddle in their white feathers,
Fence posts have white caps
Like boys, but do not move.
I cannot think why I was timid

To say I loved you, or why
I let you go eight hundred miles.
The snow has stretched the hides
Of little, white animals tight

On the sloping trunks of the trees
—the hickory we walked under
When it still had its leaves.
Days will not come again, and love

I know this too—will not suffice.
After they had been lovers tossing
Snowballs and running in the field,
After music, and after making love

In the cold, archaic light
From the snow, even two
Could not keep out the loneliness,
Would come, speechless, to the windows

As the light dies out and an evening
Too long for only making love
Hangs in their eyes. This stops me;
I do not call to say this, love,

Or break into your colored day
With this white sadness. Soon enough,
You will learn what love costs
And how it fails. The dead snow falls.

The light holds too long. A sparrow,
Shivery in his greatcoat, huddles
In the snowy, roofed, redwood feeder
For which I have run out of seed.

Taking Back

The brave little roses I got you Saturday, coming
from the dentist's in the rain
—pink, and gay soft white
in green tissue—

shed petals now which singly
drop, and drift like a circle of swans
headless in the pooling light
of the table's top.

Oh, I take them back,
in the barren weather I take them
out, crush them deep in the trash,
hoping you won't notice forever.

By the Salt Inlet

We knelt (ignoring a red sunset) on the dock
to watch translucent minnows, by the thousands,
thread the tide—rags, streamers of minnows
round the pilings, phalanxes across the opens—
and, from below, the dark darts upward,
sudden feedings bursting the shoals
to shining shrapnel, minnows leaping inches,
feet, out of the water, in all directions,
like silver grasses bent in all directions,
involuntary fountains, silver-breathy
flutings, sighing to (once more) the tide's swift
spinning circles. All up and down the inlet,
for an hour, murder was being beautiful.
Arrowy terns, with folded wings dove plopping
into the inlet, rising, death in their beaks;
and the graceful skimmers, by the marsh shore,
red-beaked, ripped seams of wake
to grasp the hording shiners. Overhead,
in lacier dyings, the swallows fought mosquitoes
high in the air. It was a circus, game,
all a carnival of flesh at frightening flesh
—reddened by sunset, golden, shadowy—
in which (to two still carnivores on the dock)
the world's feeding seemed almost an act of love.

Out of the Past

Where now the high-rise-village highways
sprawl, there was in other days
a picnic, woods, daisies, creek
you—someone?—waded, holding up a skirt.

It

could be a link of chain;
a wall, defense against
anything; a wheel
for going everywhere;
among the stars, a star, fixed;
a planet wandering; eclipsed,
a sun (rimmed with its own light);
a hoop where virgins run;
concave now, now convex,
it is a cipher next,
zero, nothing, but what
looses the multiples of thought;
a disc, crown, collar, noose;
an amphisbaena in flowers
that sweetly itself devours;
a whirlpool devouring us;
gold garland, wreath, coin, moon,
Phoenix's straw—but always mouth,
always a mouth to sing!

I wed, love, you: this ring!

Scene for a Tapestry

Blue eyes; eyes, like a sky.
The small animals of us play in the lucent groves;
    the dogs, hares.

You shall find apples in my beard, and pluck me.
There will be birds among my leaves,
    singing. Singing!

Passage

—*ark on the mountain,*
ship out of ocean;
what's in the hedgerow?
what's in the meadow?

You wake in the morning, blinking,
 and everything has to be explained:

the light to your eyes,
the red-winged blackbird eating himself
 among peach leaves (amid
 long, hooked pieces of blue sky) three
 feet out the bamboo-slit-blind window,
the noises a moment ago you hadn't heard—
 twitterings, a faraway screendoor's
 flap, rumblings, a clock,
and, in the clock's direction, the sheet-wrapped,
 turned, last night's body (sleeping)
 seeing only and hearing still in dreams
 landscaped (you? birds?) into the pillow;
and, framed through the door and the other
 room's huge window, on the inlet side,
 a motorboat right in the green
 salt grass, meadow, in the lemony morning sun,
 in the middle of a green marsh acre,
 empty, mahogany, shiny, and
 of course the birds' chittering in the air
 around it like some new kind of light, notes.

One by one, gradually, wonders—even
    the purpose of stirring, standing—
    become clear: steam of coffee, preening, world
    itself, loosed rope, tide (high, night)
    (water pushing upward to the moon),
    making love (earlier) and (earlier still)
    walking on the sunset beach . . .

Earth fits together, multiplying wonders,
    until the new day seems the same
    as all days: wonders, and the wonders
    beyond wonders (to every horizon)
    (the red-epauletted fellow still
    or again in the tree, and the groggy, pretty
    one on the pillow having coffee,
    blinking, and the boat in the meadow—
    somebody coming for it),

and you are:

you.